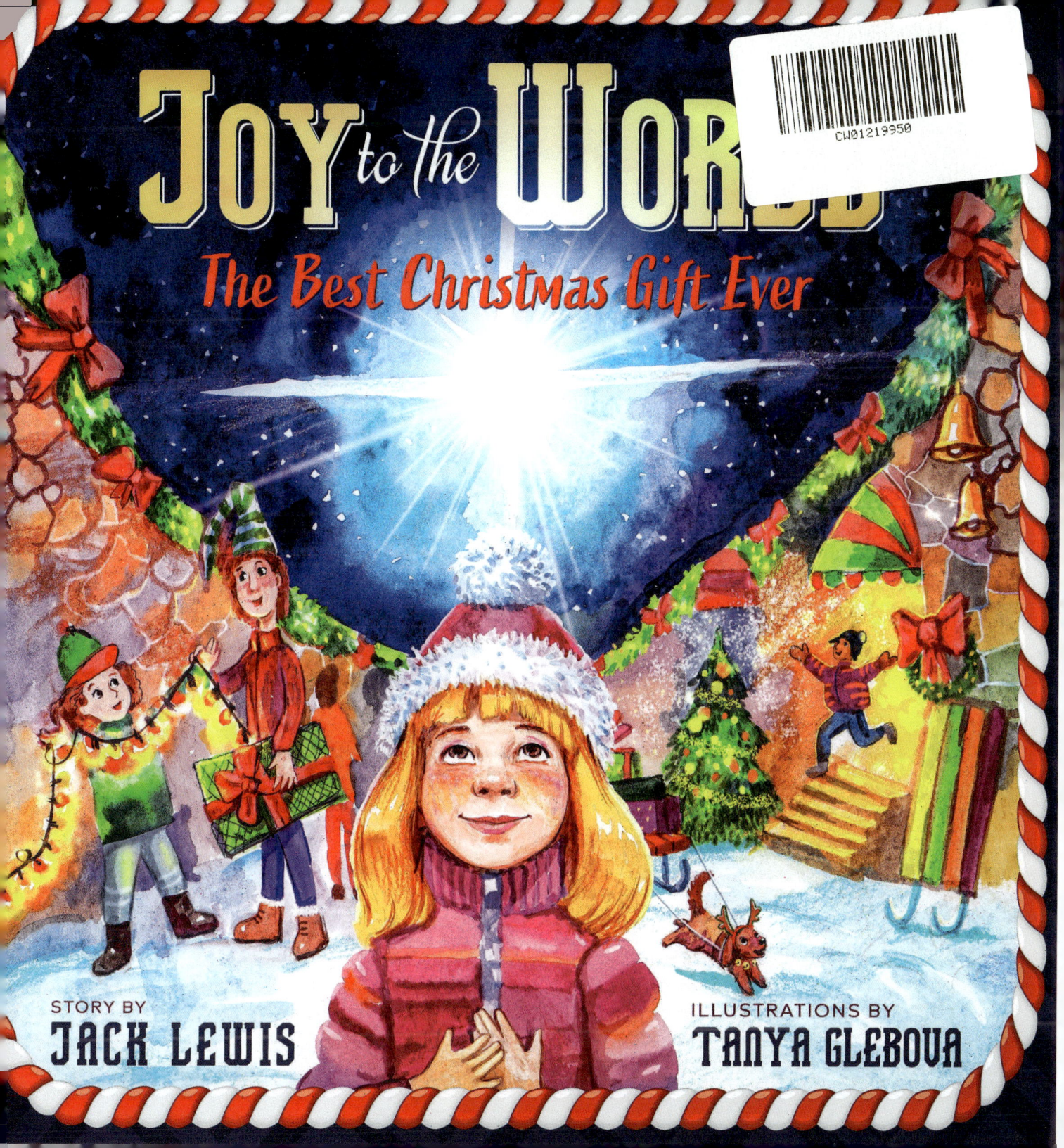

Joy to the World
The Best Christmas Gift Ever

STORY BY
JACK LEWIS

ILLUSTRATIONS BY
TANYA GLEBOVA

Dedication
For Hannah,
May Christmas always bring you smiles and joy

JOY TO THE WORLD
THE BEST CHRISTMAS GIFT EVER
Copyright © 2020 by Jack Lewis

All rights reserved. No part of this book may be used or reproduced in any manner whatsoever without written permission except in the case of brief quotations embodied in critical articles or reviews.

Thank you for buying an authorized edition of this book and for complying with copyright laws by not reproducing, scanning, or distributing any part of it in any form without permission. You are supporting writers and their hard work by doing this.

For information contact:
Starry Dreamer Publishing LLC
1603 Capitol Ave. Suite 310 A377
Cheyenne, Wyoming 82001
starrydreamerpub@gmail.com

Written by Jack Lewis
Illustrations by Tanya Glebova

ISBN: 978-1-952328-48-0 (Paperback) 978-1-952328-49-7 (Hardback)
Library of Congress Cataloging-in-Publication Data is available
10 9 8 7 6 5 4 3 2 1
First Edition: August 2020

STARRY DREAMER PUBLISHING

Christmas is a wonderful time of year, filled with many fantastic things. It is a season of excitement, expectation, and joy, but do you know the true meaning of Christmas?

When you understand what Christmas is truly about, you're able to enjoy the best Christmas gift ever!

Is Christmas all about the holiday movies and cartoons we enjoy with our family and friends?

Those holiday shows are entertaining, and it is nice to snuggle with our family to watch them, but that's not what Christmas is truly about.

Is Christmas all about the special foods, treats, and cookies we share this time of year?

Who doesn't like to make tasty Christmas cookies or gingerbread houses? It is delightful to smell yummy treats baking and it's so much fun to decorate all those cookies, but delicious food is not what Christmas is truly about.

Is Christmas all about the festive lights and decorations everywhere?

We love to hang the lights on our house and decorate our tree with beautiful, glittering ornaments. It makes our home feel cozy, cheery, and welcoming, but that's not what Christmas is truly about.

Is Christmas all about the holiday songs and carols?

Singing Christmas songs is a lot of fun! There is a lovely feeling of joy when we sing our favorite carol. Christmas music is wonderful to hear, but that's not what Christmas is truly about.

Is Christmas all about getting gifts and new toys?

Christmas morning is exciting when we wake up and find shiny, wrapped presents under our Christmas tree, but gifts that are bought from a store isn't what Christmas is truly about.

Is Christmas all about spending time with family and friends?

Sharing special time with loved ones is very important and it is the best thing we've talked about so far, but even family isn't what Christmas is truly about.

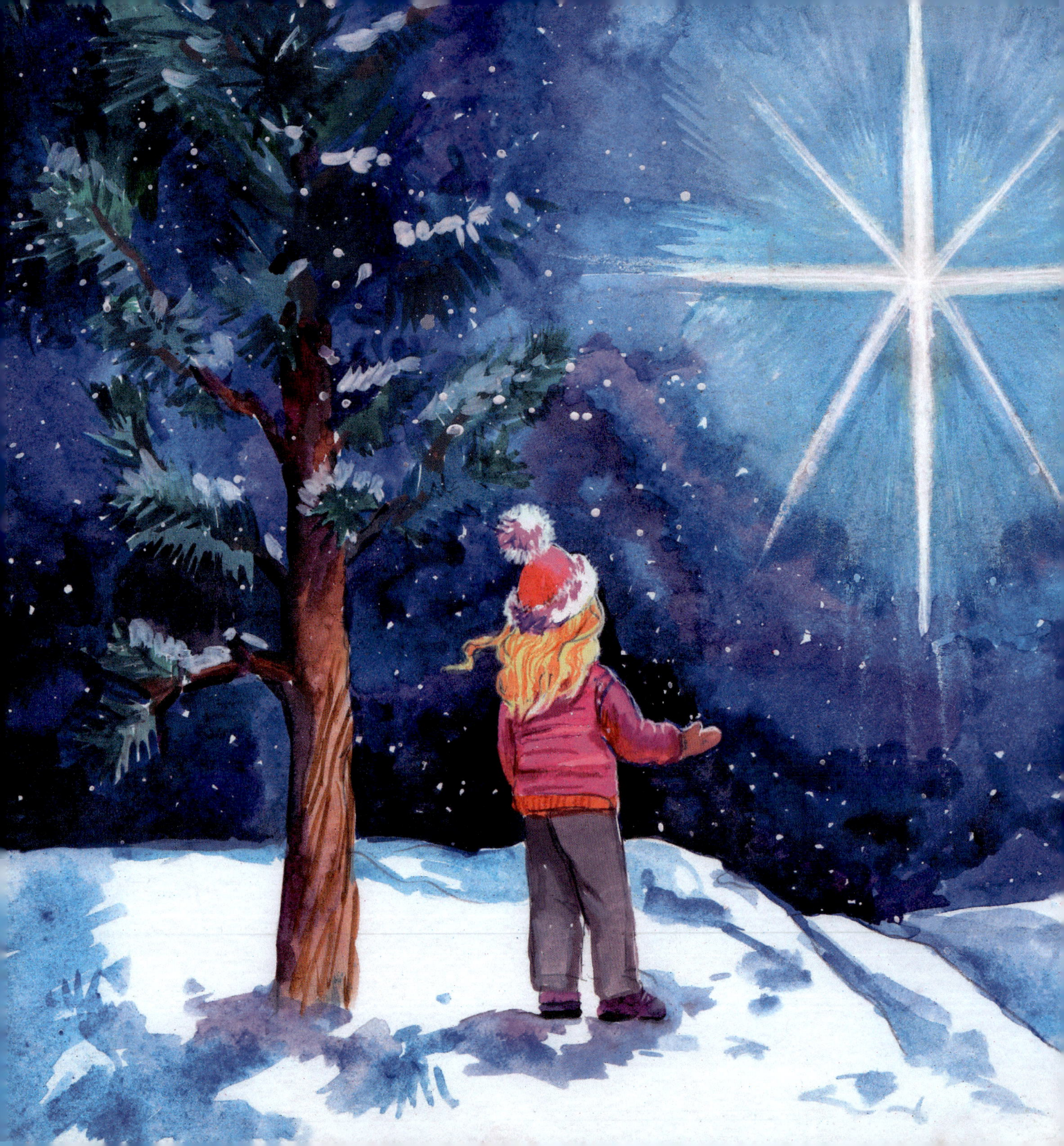

Okay then, so what is Christmas all about? What is the true meaning of Christmas?

The true meaning of Christmas is really about God's love for us! Many years ago, God sent his only son, Jesus, as a gift of love to the whole world.

He was God's special plan to save all people everywhere. Christmas is the time we remember and celebrate the birth of Jesus.

Jesus gave his life for us because he loved us so much. At Christmastime, it is good to think of God's love and to show that same kind of love to other people.

Sharing God's love and kindness is the best gift you can give anyone.

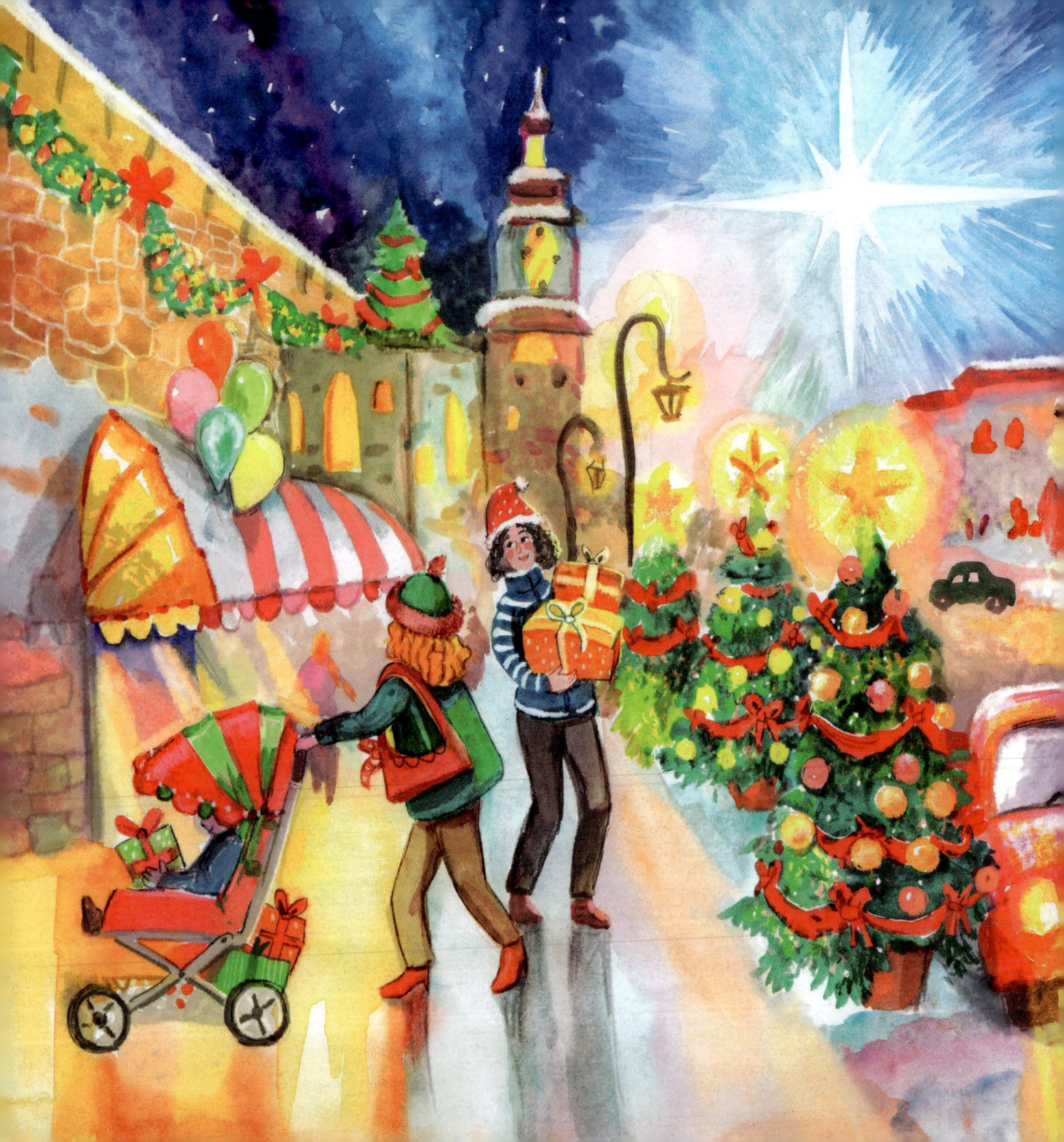

Sometimes, there is so much happening during the Christmas season that we forget about the real reason for the holiday. It is important that we take time to think about what makes Christmas special.

So have fun and celebrate this Christmas! Eat delicious cookies, sing your favorite carols, and enjoy your new toys.

Just remember to be thankful to God and to share the love of Jesus with other people.

Because that is what Christmas is truly about and **Jesus** is the best Christmas gift ever.

Merry Christmas!

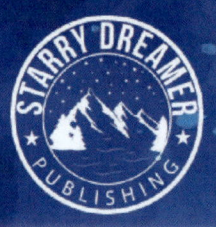

Enjoy these other great books by JACK LEWIS:

Never Bring a Zebracorn to School

Joy to the World: The Best Christmas Gift Ever

Wonderful World of Animals Series

Take a trip around the world to find the wildest, weirdest, and most adorable animals on the planet!

The Cutest Animals of the World

The Weirdest Animals of the World

The Most Dangerous Animals in the World

Today I Found… Series

Magical children's stories of friendship and the power of imagination!

Today I Found a Unicorn

Today I Found a Mermaid

Today I Found an Elf

Fun with Family Series

A wonderful way to celebrate each special person in our families!

I Love My Mommy

Printed in Great Britain
by Amazon